Praise for *Mindfulness, Mantras & Meditations*

"*Mindfulness, Mantras & Meditations* gives the reader a complete set of tools to align mind and body, and fill you with a strong sense of inner peace. Alana writes with a passion for her craft, be it meditation, poetry, mindfulness, or overall wellbeing. The underlying theme is a deep knowledge of what it means to work toward goals, and learn to accept ourselves for the beautiful, perfect, unique beings we are."

—**Velvet Spicer**,
journalist

"Alana Cahoon explores gratitude, creativity, abundance and other life-affirming forces. She also shares ideas about the challenges we all face such as "so called failures and setbacks are really detours," and "fear is a friend when it warns you." The book will help you discover balance and fulfillment, and to be grateful not only for bold achievements but for small day-to-day successes we tend to miss."

—**Scott Gudell**,
arts, entertainment & music writer/author

"This is applied mindfulness at its finest—no theory—putting mindfulness into powerful practice. Alana's wisdom pours out of the pages and into your heart and mind."

—**Fred Dewey**, growth & turnaround CEO

"This book will change your life. Alana is a life saver, literally. The most trustworthy, reliable, compassionate person I know who provides guidance and comfort like no one else. She is the one person I can trust and rely on in a crazy unreliable and ever-changing world."

—**Lily Baronas, MD**

"Alana is a trusted advisor. She is an excellent business and personal coach whom I'd highly recommend. *Mindfulness, Mantras & Meditations* offers tips that will support you in your day to day business and life."

—**Kathy Jackson**, entrepreneur

"Alana's coaching practice has been invaluable in building my business and helping manage my work-family balance. She is patient, yet purposeful, and has opened my eyes to the extreme benefits of meditation, journaling and gratitude. This book offers a glimpse into these tools. I am forever indebted!"

—**Nancy Woolver**, entrepreneur

Mindfulness, Mantras & Meditations

Mindfulness, Mantras & Meditations

*55 Inspirational Practices
to Soothe the Body, Mind & Soul*

ALANA CAHOON

Copyright © 2020 by Alana Elisabeth Cahoon

All rights reserved. This book or any portion thereof may not be reproduced or used in any manner whatsoever without the express written permission of the publisher except for the use of brief quotations in a book review or scholarly journal.

First Printing: 2020

ISBN: 978-1-7356611-0-0 (p)
ISBN: 978-1-7356611-1-7 (e)

Grow 2 B U, LLC
Rochester, NY USA

www.AlanaCahoon.com

Photography by Alana Cahoon, Chrisom B., and various artists on Pixabay.

Cover Design: Pagatana Design Service—pagatana.com
Book Interior and E-book Design: Amit Dey—amitdey2528@gmail.com
Production & Publishing Consultant: Geoff Affleck—geoffaffleck.com

OCC010000 BODY, MIND & SPIRIT / Mindfulness & Meditation
OCC019000 BODY, MIND & SPIRIT / Inspiration & Personal Growth
SEL019000 SELF-HELP / Meditations

Dedication

*To my husband,
Adam*

~

Love found

Table of Contents

Acknowledgements xiii

Introduction xvi

Chapter 1: Gratitude. 1

    Gratitude. 1

    Gratitude as Mindfulness 3

    Meditation on Appreciation 6

    Mindfulness Tip of the Day 8

    Mantra 8

Chapter 2: Physical Health. 11

    Childhood, Adolescence, Adulthood & Aging . 11

    Get Out of Your Head & Into Your Body 14

    Meditation on Your Magnificent Body. 18

    Mindfulness Tip of the Day 21

  Mantra 21

Chapter 3: Creativity 23
  See the Magic all Around You 23
  Creativity 26
  Meditations on Creative Expression 28
  Mindfulness Tip of the Day 31
  Mantra 31

Chapter 4: Anxiety 33
  It's Out There 33
  Managing Anxiety. 35
  2 Minute Meditation at the Onset of Anxiety . 37
  Mindfulness Tip of the Day 38
  Mantra 38

Chapter 5: Heartache 41
  Her Heart Ripped. 41
  The Burden of Heartache 43
  Meditation to Heal Your Heart. 43
  Mindfulness Tip of the Day 46
  Mantra 46

Chapter 6: Love 49
  Puppy Love 49

Variations of Love 52

Meditation on The Pure Essence of Love 53

Mindfulness Tip of the Day 55

Mantra 55

Chapter 7: Sleep 57

Into the Night's Calm 57

Falling Asleep Easily 59

Meditations to Sleep Peacefully 61

Mindfulness Tip of the Day 63

Mantra 63

Chapter 8: Fear Of Death 65

The Pain 65

Ashes to Ashes - Grandma Michelina 66

Meditation on Grounding, Trusting
& Preparing 70

Mindfulness Tip of the Day 72

Mantra 72

Chapter 9: Anti-Aging 75

Bear It 75

Aging Gracefully 77

Meditation—Feeling Beautiful 81

Mindfulness Tip of the Day 84

Mantra 84

Chapter 10: Abundance 87

Let It Be 87

The Power of Confidence................. 88

Meditation on Attracting Abundance........ 91

Mindfulness Tip of the Day 94

Mantra 94

About the Author 97

Acknowledgements

Through my practice of meditation and mindfulness, I am able to guide others on their paths to balance and fulfillment. I am grateful for these practices, and for my clients who have entrusted me with their hearts.

Introduction

Inspirational meditations and mantras are sprinkled throughout this book of personal development, providing creative and concrete tools to bring balance and stress reduction to your daily lives. Mindfulness training and real-life examples will assist you to understand and develop your own practice with ease.

Each chapter opens with poetry to inspire your inner muse; to awaken that creative source within; imagery to stir the soul; to reflect. Developing one's ability to reflect allows you to expand your vision and to see your world in a different light. You may even be inspired to take out a pen and paper and write your own poem.

The commentary following is filled with mindfulness training, and provides unique ways to continue expanding that viewpoint. You will find that reconnecting with your body will improve your ability to focus; that adding Epsom salt to your bath will aide you in sound sleep;

that noticing the colors within a painting will ignite your creativity.

Mindfulness training is recognized throughout the professional community as the leading tool to manage stress at the workplace. It is also found to bring peace at home. Meditation and mindfulness techniques can be used to clear the mind, release the past, and attain goals.

As you turn the pages within this book, you may enjoy the following benefits:

- Increased joy and happiness
- Reduced stress and anxiety
- Improved clarity and focus
- Access to intuition and creativity
- Increased vitality and health
- Inner peace and calm

You will learn how to:

- Meditate to quiet the mind and relax the body
- Use meditation to serve your overall health and happiness
- Develop techniques to attract abundance
- Use mantras to support your well-being and attain goals
- Reflect on the hidden meanings of life and to be inspired by them

- Develop a mindfulness practice
- Be present in the moment
- Maintain a sense of calm amidst a storm

Each chapter leads you in one or more guided meditations or creative visualizations to bring clarity around the topic. These step-by-step meditations are easy to follow and may be repeated as long as you like.

The Mindfulness Tip of the Day is the collective nugget of wisdom gained throughout each chapter. These are fun to carry with you throughout the day.

Your mantra is a powerful phrase to affirm that you have gained this wisdom and knowledge. By repeating it whenever you can, you strengthen its reality within you.

It gives me great pleasure to share these words of inspiration. My intention is to bring a sense of serenity to your life; to empower you to live a life of purpose and joy.

With Loving Kindness ~

Alana

Chapter 1

GRATITUDE

GRATITUDE

Each day I awake
I offer thanks
For the warmth of my bed
The comfort of home
The kindness of family

Each day I look around
And give thanks
For the beauty of the trees, the flowers
and the rolling hills
The clouds in the sky
The birds singing their song
Life passing along

Each evening I give thanks
For the food set in front of me

To nurture my body
The time to reflect and calm my mind

Each night I lie in bed
And give thanks
For the extraordinary opportunity to live another day
To move in my miraculous body
To energize it with wholesome foods
To engage it in physical activity
To purify it inside and out with water

With the power of the mind
To illuminate kindness
To pacify anger
To heal pain
To open to the possibility
Of doing it all again
On a new day if I'm so lucky

GRATITUDE AS MINDFULNESS

Gratitude is one of the simplest forms of Mindfulness. Maybe in its simplicity, it is often missed. We grow accustomed to the way things are, and simply expect them to continue.

But this is not always so.

Life has a way of shaking things up. Have you noticed? Just when things are really looking up. A detour here. A detour there.

Gratitude helps you to stay on track. To appreciate when life is moving along at a steady hum. When your meals are prepared and served and easily digested.

It helps you to see the glass half full.

Thankfulness is especially helpful during times of stress.

Give this some thought.

When was the last time you found yourself complaining? Even today. Simply look back and review what it was that you were unhappy about. Then examine the situation. Did it cause you grief? Physical injury? Confusion? Did it set off a series of what ifs? How did this moment go from nothing to something. Something worth complaining about?

There are no wrong choices here. No judgments being made. Simply an observation and reflection—maybe even an analysis of what could possibly cause you unhappiness.

As you look more closely at any given situation that may not fit in with the norm, you may begin to find that the issue wasn't as detrimental as first thought.

Here is an example.

This morning I ran out of coffee and didn't have time to stop at a cafe to pick up a cup of java. Irritated and not quite awake, I continued on to my appointment only to realize that I had forgotten the documents I had prepared the night before.

Frustrated, I found myself blaming my poor husband for not telling me he had used the last cup of coffee. After all, if my morning routine hadn't gotten interrupted, I wouldn't have forgotten my papers.

It's how we respond to the curves that are important

Practicing mindfulness allowed me to pay mind to my emotions, validating them without adding judgment or blame to myself or others. Things happen when we least expect them. It's how we respond to the curves that are important. In this case, instead of getting upset, I could have looked for an alternative to coffee such as brewing a hot cup of strong black tea.

Mindfulness also offered me the opportunity to be creative at the meeting. I may not have had the printed materials but I was prepared. The missing cup of coffee was a perfect way to begin, with an imperfect human story.

When you find yourself in a similar situation, pause, acknowledge, and detach yourself from the emotions percolating. Use these distractions as a way to be creative, spontaneous, real.

In the end, that's what we all want. To sit across the table from someone who is authentic.

Use the curves in the road as reminders to not take the ease of life for granted. But to receive such detours as opportunities to be resourceful. To be real.

Gratitude allows you to see the bright light in all situations, no matter how dire they may appear. See the glass half full, and it will always be half full.

*Gratitude is one of the simplest forms
of Mindfulness*

MEDITATION ON APPRECIATION

Close your eyes and take 5 deep breaths in and out. With each breath in, expand your chest and diaphragm. With each breath out, drop your shoulders and sink into your cushion.

Offer gratitude

Beginning at the top of your head. Give thanks. For your hair, your eyes, your nose, mouth and jaw.

Moving down your neck and throat. Give thanks. To and for your entire body for its exquisite nature and ability to move and function.

Relax

Give thanks for the miracle of your mind. Its ability to read and process material such as this.

Relax

Give thanks to your imagination. Its complexities bringing color to your world.

Breathe

Offer gratitude for the basics being taken care of. A warm bed. A safe home. A hot meal.

Take a moment now to reflect on a meaningful relationship. Someone whom you can count on. To be there in times of need. To show up and celebrate your successes.

Be grateful

Take a long deep breath in and a slow breath out. Bring your focus to your breath. Offer thanks. For the breath of life.

MINDFULNESS TIP OF THE DAY

Throughout the day stop and give thanks. For whatever is around you. For both the obvious opportunities for joy and perhaps the less obvious.

- Give thanks every time you smile. Notice the source.
- Appreciate your many achievements throughout the day. Whether small or big.
- See everything as an opportunity to be grateful for.

Notice how it magnifies. The more you give thanks, the more you will have to be grateful for!

MANTRA

"The more I give thanks, the more
I will have to be grateful for."

JOURNAL YOUR INSIGHTS

EVEN GETTING A LITTLE BIT DONE CAN BE SEEN AS AN ACCOMPLISHMENT.

Chapter 2

PHYSICAL HEALTH

CHILDHOOD, ADOLESCENCE, ADULTHOOD & AGING

Josh
It's 6:00 in the morning and I can't wait to get up!
There's snow on the ground
And Dad says we're going to build a snowman
Mom says she'll teach us how to make snow angels
I thought angels flew in the sky

Gary
Alarm rings
It's 6 AM. Ugh. I can't get up
I don't want to get up
Do I have to get up? Ugh
The bus shows up in less than an hour
I don't even like coffee

But I guess I'll try it
Everyone else seems to like it
And there's that cute girl who hangs out in
the cafe after school
Latte ... cafe ... late
"I'll have a Latte please. Add some syrup to it."
If she's cute - the girl pouring the drink—barista? Yeah
I'll tell her to pick the syrup
… Man, did I grow again overnight?
My pants don't fit
They're too short!

Donna
I love working out at the gym
I love working out at the gym
I love working out at the gym
If I keep telling myself this, I will start to believe it
This is my new mantra
OK
Why do they make these 'yoga pants' so tight?
I swear they shrink every time I wash them
Bra. Which bra to wear … the purple one
Is that in style now?
Breathe ... just breath
I hear meditation is good now
Whatever that means
I just want to lose some weight
Get back into those hot girl jeans

I love working out
I love working out
God I hate this. Somebody just give
me a doughnut. Or a new body

Leah
It's 9:00? How did it get so late?
I need to go to bed or I'll never get up in the morning
But then I'll just lie there
Thinking
Maybe I should stretch
But my body aches
How did it get so out of shape?
There are those weights in the corner of the room
I keep saying I'm going to use them
But they're too heavy
And I'm too old
Maybe a glass of wine will help
I'm not supposed to drink wine any more
It upsets my stomach
I'm tired ... bored ... cranky
And I just don't care
What's the use
I know I'll try again tomorrow

Joseph
Oh my
I don't need that walker

Can't you see I'm fine
Honestly
You'd think I was 100 years old
I've got eight to go!
Get out of my way
I can do this on my own
Kids

GET OUT OF YOUR HEAD & INTO YOUR BODY

There's this great song that opens with 'Girl look at my body. I work out.' The music video is humorous, making light of the situation. The singer actually looks out of shape, but is thinking about getting into shape, because if he was in shape, he'd get the hot babe. Or so he thinks.

We often take our bodies for granted. And don't notice them until something changes. A gray hair. A love handle. An ache or pain. Or a new love interest.

*Wouldn't it be wonderful to live in that
ever-present moment of childhood*

Wouldn't it be wonderful to live in that ever-present moment of childhood. Where every day you wake up and jump out of bed to play. Whether it's in the snow or on the beach. Exercise is an intrinsic part of your childhood physical development. And it's fun!

Then we grow up. We get all caught up in our head, and forget about our bodies. They're there. They'll always be there. We take them for granted.

We ignore our true physical needs. And too often abuse them. It may be:

Sugar

"Those cookies are so good. I'll just have one more."

Boredom

"What do you want to do?" "I don't know."

"Let's go out to eat."

"OK."

Loneliness

"Do you want to come home with me?"

"Maybe. We only just met. What will we do?"

"Hang out."

"But aren't you seeing someone else?"

"Yeah. But we're in an open relationship."

Exhaustion

"Give me some more of that coffee! I don't care if it's 1:00 in the morning. My doctor doesn't know what she's talking about anyway. I'm gonna push-push-push till I get it done-done-done!"

Pressure

"Are you hungry? Eat some more."

"I already ate. I'm good."

"You're skinny as a rail. Eat."

"All right. All right"

Too busy

"I have no time for exercise. Are you kidding me? Did you see this pile on my desk? That was due yesterday."

Reasons to ignore our bodies are endless. But here are the reasons to pay attention.

- Vitality
- Relaxation

- Longevity
- Happiness
- Self Respect
- Health
- Sleep

These may look similar to the reasons you ignore your body. But they're not. Consuming alcohol may numb your mind but does not assist in sleep. Eating cookies may give you an initial high but will soon become your low. Caffeine appears to wake you up but Vitamin C will really do the trick. Casual sex may seem

gratifying, but it is in truly connecting in a loving manner called intimacy when you will feel satiated.

The following meditation will help you to reconnect with your body. To get 'out of your head'. Physical health begins here.

MEDITATION ON YOUR MAGNIFICENT BODY

Meditation #1 Relaxation

Sit in a quiet place with your back straight but comfortable.

Close your eyes. Take 5 deep breaths in and out. With each breath, relax your body, and drop into your cushion.

Bring your awareness to your head. Imagine there is a golden sun above you. Feel the rays of light pouring over you. Relaxing all the muscles in your head. Massaging your forehead. Relaxing the inner corners of your eyes. And the outer corners of your eyes.

Take a deep breath in and a long breath out. Feel the light pour over your face. Relaxing your jaw. All the muscles in your neck and throat.

Imagine beams of light pouring over your shoulders. Down your arms and hands.

Bring your awareness to the crown of your head. Visualize your sun. And feel it sending healing light down the front of your body. Down your back. Golden light pooling around your feet. You are completely relaxed.

Meditation #2 Physical Health

Bring your awareness to your hands. Wiggle your fingers. Then relax.

Reflect on all the ways you use your hands. Typing. Washing dishes. Driving. Cooking. Holding a friend's hand. Bathing. Gardening. Painting. Sewing. Dribbling a ball.

Offer gratitude for all the things your loving hands do for you. Honor them. Set your intention to massage them with hand lotion. Mindfully.

Bring your awareness to your feet. Imagine the golden sun above your head sending a beam of light down around your feet. Bathing them in a pool of light. Wiggle your toes.

Think about how your feet serve you. How they carry you throughout the day. Taking you from one place to the next. What do you wear on your feet? Are they comfortable? Supportive? Stylish? How do you care for your feet? See yourself doing that now. Getting a pedicure. Reflexology. Wearing good shoes.

Breathe in. And out. Bring your awareness to your spine. Think about how it serves you. Moving you from one direction to the other. Whether side to side or up and down. Admire its versatility!

Now imagine the light streaming down from the top of your spine to the bottom. Healing every vertebrae. Limbering. Your spine. Sending rays out throughout your entire back. Relaxing and revitalizing every muscle. Honor it with a massage.

See the light above you flowing down the front of your body. Bring your awareness to your abdomen. See it rise and fall with each breath.

Imagine the incredible process going on right now inside your belly! Digestion. This miraculous internal body of yours never sleeps. It is always on call. Clearing out the old. And bringing in the new. Breathe into your abdomen and assist in this natural process. Affirm that you will nurture your body.

See yourself as a body of light. Completely surrounded by golden rays. Healing. Relaxing. Renewing.

Offer yourself LOVE. Nurturing love. Reconnect with your true nature. Your elaborate body Your beautiful magnificent body.

MINDFULNESS TIP OF THE DAY

Before making decisions regarding your body whether it is eating, sleeping, drinking, clothing or engaging in sexual activity, pause. Consider what you truly want. Whether it's companionship or a good night's sleep. Offer it a healthy alternative such as exercise, meditation, a solid meal, a glass of water, a walk or talk with a friend. Marvel at your body's intricacies and beauty.

Marvel at your body's intricacies and beauty

MANTRA

"I now am aware of how my body serves me.
I nurture my body with loving kindness."

JOURNAL YOUR INSIGHTS

Chapter 3

CREATIVITY

SEE THE MAGIC ALL AROUND YOU

Perusing cafes
In the village
Priming the future
Cafe Reggio
Washington Square Park
Looking into candle flames
Wondering where & when we'd meet
Longing for romance

Sipping roasts from around the world
You'd think this poem was about coffee
Coffee ... sex ... music ... art
They all went hand in hand
All leading to romance
I was an extreme romantic

I fell in love with the city
I hated the city
I fell in love with jazz
I hated the jazz scene
I fell in love with spirituality
I am still a seeker
Waiting to be found

My inspiration came from
My cafes
The few that existed then
I found them
In every crevice ... enclave ... neighborhood
Spooning out cockroaches
Laughing with girlfriends
Writing endless entries in my personal journals

I would look up and be certain it was you
Looking into your stunning eyes
Captivating smile
Until your gaze passed mine
Or clutched so intensely that I dropped my own

Love ... music ... art ... galleries
Soho ... Greenwich Village ... the stage
All is lost
Now
In adulthood

The maturation of time
Leading to the answer
Found love
Searching for the match
To relight the flame
That years of raising children have put out
But let's not blame it on them

Poor littles ones
Apples of our eyes
The flame is always burning within
The match never out of reach

Breathe
In and out
See
The magic
All around you
Feel the light of the heavens
Embrace you
Paint
Sing
Write
Art
Love
Now

CREATIVITY

Wow. I haven't written like that since, well, before kids. Before the mother syndrome kicked in and called off all other shows for me. I was a mother now. The most important job I'd ever have. Whew. Thank God they've grown up. It's time for me again. For that romantic. The woman who loved to travel and explore cultures. Gaze at their art. Listen to their music. And drink their coffees!

Inspiration comes in a variety of forms. What's important is to identify yours. Where? When? How? What are you doing? There are so many questions to bring you along the journey of creativity.

Often there are blocks. These may show up as limiting beliefs i.e. 'I'm not interesting. No one wants to hear me sing. I don't have any talent. My brother's the one who can draw.'

Or time. 'There just isn't enough time in the day to paint any more, design any more, play the violin anymore.'

Many of us live in a world of chaos

And the latter may be true. Many of us live in a world of chaos with lists longer than the hours of the day. Time management skills may help—a little. Letting go of items on the list—yes. Moving through each day with grace and gratitude—definitely. Bringing yourself home to your inspiration—a must.

And those limiting beliefs. Most likely picked up along the way. Can all be dropped. Erased from your memory. Released from your energy field.

Creativity is like a stream. One that is either flowing or damned up. You've all heard of writer's block. That's the stream that is damned!

Here are some ways to unclog your stream if stuck.

MEDITATIONS ON CREATIVE EXPRESSION

Meditation # 1 Art

Go to an art gallery, and truly look at a painting. You don't need to be an artist. You need to see! Notice the variety of colors. Are they vibrant? Or dull? What is the most used color?

What is the theme of the picture? Are there people involved? Animals? Nature?

How does it make you feel? Happy? Sad? Nothing at all?

Where does your eye go? To a corner of the portrait? The center? A figure or color?

How does it inspire you? Do you want to get your paints out and create your own work of art? Do you find yourself humming a tune? Is there an itch to write your thoughts out?

Meditation # 2 Nature

Go for a walk in nature. Find a place to sit and rest by an actual stream of water. Watch the ripples move around rocks. Listen to the flow. Breathe in deeply and smell the earthiness of the air. Allow your mind to reflect on the calming nature of the stream. Bringing your thoughts to the forefront. What are you thinking? How do these thoughts serve you? Do they stimulate your brain? Or drain your brain? Do they nourish your soul? Or deplete it? After closer examination, toss these thoughts into the stream and watch them float away, waving good-bye.

Look up to the sky and open your mind to the freedom of new ideas. Those that inspire you into your greatness. Whether it's completing the project in your basement or opening the jar to a new endeavor, be inspired to the creativity within you!

Meditation # 3 Writing

Coffee! Today there are so many cafes to choose from. I'm in NYC now and have a choice of 5 'coffee shops' within a 2-block radius. When I lived here over 20 years ago that would have looked more like 1 cafe in a 12-block radius. Not including Bodegas!

Find your way to a cafe—by yourself. You're allowed a newspaper, book or digital device of your choice but also bring along a pen and paper.

Get your favorite hot beverage. Teas are nice, too! And relax. Mindfulness training reminds you to pause. To be observant. To not only look but to see. Try that now—if you are in a cafe. Notice everything! The walls—their color and texture, what's hanging on them. Is there a theme? I.e. Do you notice photos of bread being made? Flowers in baskets? Coffee beans being harvested?

What are the sounds? Do you hear a cappuccino machine frothing fresh milk? People talking? Music being streamed in the background?

What are the smells? Are they heavenly? Breads? Dark roasts?

What do you feel? Are there people around? Do you feel comfortable? Are you self-conscious?

Take out your paper and write your responses down. All of them. Without judgment. You have just been creative!

MINDFULNESS TIP OF THE DAY

Opening to your creativity often begins with being inspired. It also helps to remove mental blocks that may be getting in your way.

Allow these moments of inspiration to unblock the currents of your creativity

Explore your mind to discover ways that inspire you, whether it's gazing into an art-piece, taking a walk in nature, or going to a cafe by yourself with pen in hand. Allow these moments of inspiration to unblock the currents of your creativity and then act upon them! Complete an unfinished project. Write down a clever idea. Make someone laugh at a joke you made up. Dust off the guitar and sing.

MANTRA

"I now open to the stream of creativity that is flowing within me. I am inspired by art, nature and coffee."
(replace these with your sources of inspiration)

JOURNAL YOUR INSIGHTS

Chapter 4

ANXIETY

IT'S OUT THERE

Anger
Who's out there?
How dare they!
Who do they think they are?!

Fear
Knowing something's out there
Something's not safe
The unknown

Uncertainty is the greatest fear alive
If you let it live

And what happens when you do know
What is out there
How do you keep it at bay
How do you keep it out of here

Away from you
Away from your loved ones?

Emotions
Will rattle you every time

I KNOW IT'S OUT THERE!

Your breathing becomes panting
Shallow
Your chest tightens
You clench your fists
Your jaw

Danger
Fight or Flight
What to do

Breathe
Deeply
Slowly
Until your confidence comes back
And your demons disappear

MANAGING ANXIETY

Anxiety has been crippling society over the past 4 decades. As we become connected on a 24/7 basis, our brains and emotions are on alert. Nearly 24/7. This creates havoc in our mental state and physical body.

We aren't computers. We aren't digital (yet!). We are human beings with physical needs and limitations. Such as sleep and down time.

<u>Our emotional state has been affected with 'friends' whom we've never truly met. Whom we know nothing about.</u> Their name, address and sex could all be a farce.

Fear. It used to be obvious. Be afraid of the dark because an angry animal may be hungry or simply annoyed and the last thing you need is to be in his or her way. Be scented on their track.

But now, it is different. Even the fear of getting in the way of an angry person is getting pushed aside. Now it's social media. Being connected to possibly untrustworthy individuals or groups.

Being on 24/7 also means, well, that you're on 24/7! You may be answering emails at midnight, feeding your children at 6 AM and rushing to get to the office by 7. Only to come home at 6 PM—if you're lucky—put the dinner on, get the kids to bed, and so on. It's a pervasive circle that may eventually crush you.

You may find yourself having a panic attack. What is that anyway? Physically your chest tightens and you fight for air. Emotionally you're overwhelmed, frightened, paralyzed. Usually without an answer. You usually do not know what the source is. Because of brain fatigue. You're overworked, spend excessive time on social media, and may have developed an addiction.

Create a path of action to heal
Create a sense of serenity

So, how to help prevent anxiety. How to determine the original source. And how to create a path of action to heal and to create a sense of serenity.

2 MINUTE MEDITATION AT THE ONSET OF ANXIETY

Admit that you are beginning to feel anxiety.

Do not try to push it away.

Breathe into it by taking a deep breath in and long breath out.

Give the anxiety a name. George. Cindy. Carol. Nut-head. Anything.

Then ask it what it's trying to tell you.

'What do you want, Gary?'

And treat it like a friend. Remember, fear is your friend when it is warning you of something truly dangerous.

And then just wait.

Breathe.

Until you get an answer. Or not.

Then thank it for keeping an eye out for you.

And say good-bye.

MINDFULNESS TIP OF THE DAY

Fear is created out of the unknown. Fear can be your friend. Seek out the source. Make the changes necessary to remove the source from your life. Bring in peace and calm. Breathe.

MANTRA

"When anxiety arises, I pay attention,
and ask what message it has for me.
Then thank it, and let it go."

JOURNAL YOUR INSIGHTS

Chapter 5

HEARTACHE

HER HEART RIPPED

She felt lonely
Isolated
No one could hear her
Of course, she stopped singing
Speaking ... Had she lost her voice?

Pain ... to release it would, well, hurt
To sing would open the valve to a flowing of tears
She closed her eyes and felt
The pain in her heart
Empty
Her entire body was hallowed out
She was nothing but a pile of bones
A skeleton
Her heart ripped

Out
A torn piece of fabric
Red silk
With a stake in it
Not even a good one
A lousy golf tee
That's all her love was worth
And it was misplaced
Now hanging on the right side of her chest
Closer to her shoulder
Emptiness
Nothing left

To feel
To love

THE BURDEN OF HEARTACHE

There's nothing worse than feeling the heaviness of heartache. Like a burden you're trudging around with.

Loneliness. There are a million songs about it. It tugs at your soul. It affects your mind process. You become obsessed with thoughts of melancholy and revenge!

Thich Nhat Hahn writes about the art of suffering. Rather the art of managing our pain. Because in truth it may not go away. But you can learn to tolerate it, and keep it at bay.

MEDITATION TO HEAL YOUR HEART

Calm your body, mind and emotions with 9 relaxing breaths, breathing in fresh clean air, breathing out and letting go.

Bring to the forefront of your mind heartache. Remembering a time, a person, or an experience that hurt you. See it in front of you as if it were on a screen. Then close your eyes and breathe deeply into your heart chakra located in the center of your chest.

Feel the sensation that the heartache brings to you physically. Allow it. Don't fight it. It is in allowing the emotion that we can look it straight in the eye, deal with it, and let it go.

Notice how the emotion of the pain makes you feel. Do you feel hallowed out like a skeleton? Is there a stake pierced in your heart? Has your heart been ripped out and torn? Describe it.

Take a deep breath in and release the experience. Just let it drop away for the moment.

Bring your awareness to your breath. Watching your breath flow in and out. Feeling the rise and fall of your ribcage and abdomen. Relax.

Now, bringing your awareness back to your heart center or chakra, imagine a golden light, like a star or the sun. Feel it ignite within you as you breathe. A gentle glowing star resting in the center of your heart. Focus on this for several breaths.

*A gentle glowing star resting in the center
of your heart*

Then bring the memory of the pain you were working with before. See it as it appeared to you. Notice it's color, shape, and sensation. And place it in the very center of your golden light. Allow the light to heal your pain. Imagine it has incredible healing powers! Feel it dissolve the heartache until only the light is shining.

You may ask for a symbol from this light to keep in your heart to protect you from further pain. Or to assist you in managing dealings of the heart. See what appears for you. Hold it in the presence of the golden light, and integrate it with your heart energy.

Come back to the present moment feeling a sense of peace and understanding. An incredible healing has taken place.

MINDFULNESS TIP OF THE DAY

When you go throughout the day, notice how you respond to life. Then check within. Place your hands over your heart chakra, and ask yourself how you're feeling. This will give you a deeper understanding of your responses to life, allowing you to make more informed choices.

MANTRA

"I open my heart to love with a new sense of trust and understanding."

JOURNAL YOUR INSIGHTS

Chapter 6

LOVE

PUPPY LOVE

She wrapped her arms around him
Filled with love
She breathed deeply into the center of her heart
Feeling the boundless depths of love
Breathing out, she poured that love like streams of intoxicating energy
Into and around her pup, her sweet, cuddly dog
Creating a boundless connection
Never to be forgotten

Retreating she pondered the question of love
How could she love her dog this closely and yet no other
Was it simply safe?
Did she know he would always be there
Always ready to follow

To lead
To play
To be
To snuggle at her feet throughout the night

Love
Like a current of the wind
Blowing through you
Filling that void
Nurturing your soul
Comforting your mind
Like no other feeling
Healing
Kind
Unending
Sometimes hidden
But
Always there

Love
Be brave
To love yet another
Trusting
That he or she may wander off
But remain alive
Like a star in the sky
In your heart

Alana Cahoon

VARIATIONS OF LOVE

Love is the essence of happiness.

Love is the essence of happiness

It's true. If you have ever felt it, like a warm flow of nectar, you will know that it's true.

But love comes in many forms.

There's romance. Which is wrought with highs and lows. Especially if it takes form as passion.

There's friendship which one would like to believe is steady and balanced. It usually is. It's a kindred love of companionship.

There's parental love for a child and vice versa. This for me is the most precious. To care for one who is at the beginning of self-discovery and world exploration. And their love for you. That fond adoration.

The most important love of all begins within. This is not narcissism. It is recognizing the self as an expression of the Divine. Once we learn how to love ourselves exactly as we are, to nurture ourselves as we would our children, to respect ourselves as we should our elders, and treat ourselves as we would our best friends, we will have built a solid foundation to attract and maintain loving and meaningful relationships with others.

Recognize the self as an expression of the Divine

MEDITATION ON THE PURE ESSENCE OF LOVE

Take 3 deep breaths in and long breaths out. Clearing out your head. Calming your emotions. And relaxing your body.

Bring your awareness to the center of your heart chakra, in the very center of your chest.

Breathe into this space. Watching the ribcage expand and settle.

Imagine a golden light resting here like a star.

As you breathe into it, imagine your breath igniting the light within you.

Now think of someone or thing or even a place that brings you joy. That you really love. See that person or what you've chosen resting in the center of your golden star. See the light gleam around it.

Close your eyes if they are open and breathe deeply into your heart feeling the essence of love.

What does it feel like?
Does it have a color? A sound?
Does it have a verb?
An adjective?
Breathe into this feeling and imagine it spreading throughout your entire body.

Now imagine that you are standing in front of a mirror.
See yourself filled with glowing light.
Beaming with the essence of love.
Stay centered. Just be aware of the mirrored image of you.

Now say to your self.
I love myself.
I love my life.
I love my friends and family.
I love my world.
I love the feeling of love.

Let the mirror dissolve.
Allow yourself to rest in the pure essence of love.

MINDFULNESS TIP OF THE DAY

Catch yourself when thoughts of anger or depression arise. Return to yourself, bringing your awareness to your heart chakra, and remember a time, a person or a place that truly made you happy. Breathe it deeply within and know that that feeling is your birthright. It is your choice to experience amid all situations.

MANTRA

"As I love and accept myself,
I experience the essence of love."

JOURNAL YOUR INSIGHTS

Chapter 7

SLEEP

INTO THE NIGHT'S CALM

The pillow was soft and puffy
Her blanket lined with satin
The sheets warm and snug
Sigh
Snuggling in the warmth of night
Window slightly ajar
Gentle breeze floating
Like musical notes
Ahh
Cocooned in
To a fabric swath
Silently taking her away
Into the night's calm
Land of dreams

Fairytales
Make believe
Sweet sweet dreams

FALLING ASLEEP EASILY

The poem nearly lulls you to sleep. The mind creating a journey into the pleasures of dreamland. Sleep.

But this is not always accessible. After a long day of work, the mind may be drained. One might think it would be the perfect remedy to sleep. But being overtired can sometimes do just the opposite. You may instead find yourself exhausted and wide awake.

There are a number of obstacles that may get in the way of you and a peaceful night of sleep. Being overtired is only one of them.

Worry is another. Emotions focused on negative outcomes rarely induce restful sleep. You've probably heard the phrase, 'I was up all night worried.' In fact, you may have said it yourself!

An active mind with to-do lists that still need checking off can be an eye-opener at bedtime. And the creative mind coming up with new ideas, as clever as they may be, does not promote sound sleep.

Certain foods and beverages can wreak havoc on falling asleep. Sugars are top culprits. And medicines are notorious for interrupting your sleeping patterns.

So, what does one do to get a good night's sleep? Here are a few ways to assist your body, mind and spirit to wind down for the day and prepare for sleep.

What's soothing to the body is soothing to the soul

Herbal Tea

Hot tea is soothing to the body. And what's soothing to the body is soothing to the soul. Select herbs that you like. Chamomile is known to calm nerves as well as digestion and may be a good choice. A drop of honey is a natural sweetener for your beverage.

Hot Bath

Adding Epsom salt to your bath assists in relaxing your muscles. This aids your body in the relaxing process needed to fall asleep. Light a candle and play soothing music to add ambience.

Essential Oils

Lavender has a calming effect and is often used to help people relax. Spray a mixture upon your pillow or room or keep a dried sprig nearby. You can also apply a drop of pure essential oil onto your wrist. Or into your bath.

MEDITATIONS TO SLEEP PEACEFULLY

Meditating clears the mind. What may be keeping you awake is having an active one. Do you remember the childhood remedy of counting sheep? Meditating can be similar. Here are a few meditations to try.

Meditation #1 Counting the Breath

You can literally count the breath from 1 - 10 saying to yourself the number such as 'one' upon the exhale and continuing to 'ten'. Once you're done, start at the top and repeat. If you get lost, return to 'one'. Add a visual to the count if you'd like. For instance, visualize a new flower blossoming with each breath. Or see the numbers as you count.

Meditation #2 Body Scan

Bring your awareness to each part of your body beginning with your head, and imagine it relaxing. For instance, as you bring your awareness to your eyes, say to yourself, "My eyes are now resting."

This relaxation meditation is a great precursor to all meditations, allowing you to be fully present. In this case, preparing you to sleep!

Meditation #3 Gratitude

Count your blessings

Counting your blessings is a wonderful way to give thanks and to reflect on the good things in life. Simplify by recognizing one blessing that occurred to you that day, or something you are grateful for.

When you feel happy, you are more likely to fall asleep with ease. Your dreams may be more colorful. And you'll wake feeling refreshed.

Meditation #4 Forgiveness

This is similar to gratitude. When we forgive ourselves and others, we free ourselves, creating harmony in our lives including our sleep.

MINDFULNESS TIP OF THE DAY

Prepare yourself for sound sleep ahead of time. Select a relaxing activity like drinking a cup of hot herbal tea or taking a luxurious bath. Follow this with a soothing meditation to clear the mind and calm the emotions. Say your mantra.

Good night

MANTRA

"I fall asleep with ease. I am calm.
I am relaxed."

JOURNAL YOUR INSIGHTS

Chapter 8

FEAR OF DEATH

THE PAIN

Shrinking back from the idea of it
He walked away
Not knowing where to go
What to do
Someone—he loved—was dying

The pain was too much for him to bear
He wasn't the one dying
It didn't make sense
And yet, here he was, dying his own death
inside his own mind

It felt
It felt
Like he couldn't bear it any more
He needed to run away

He couldn't
No matter where he went
The thought haunted him
Am I next?
Where will I go?
Who will be near me?
What will happen?

And with that
He went home
And cried

ASHES TO ASHES - GRANDMA MICHELINA

From ashes to ashes. I grew up with that phrase. Being blessed every spring during the ceremony of Ash Wednesday. The priest would place ashes upon our foreheads, reminding us that although we were here now, someday we wouldn't be.

It represented the first day of Lent, commemorating the 40 days that the Christian prophet, Jesus went off in silent retreat. The Holy Week that follows is in memory of his death and resurrection.

And so, death is not a new concept. It is approached as a main theme in many faiths. Growing up in the Roman Catholic Church, I attended many funeral services, beginning with my grandmother's, Michelina Donnatelli Ventura. I loved her so much. But I wasn't scared when I awoke to find her dead.

She was beautiful, with long flowing silver hair

Grandma Michelina used to watch me. I loved staying with her! She only spoke Italian, and although I only spoke English, I seemed to understand every word. I remember waking to the smell of eggs being scrambled on the stovetop with bread baking in the oven. She was beautiful, with long flowing silver hair that she wound up in a bun on the back of her head. She was always smiling and singing.

On that morning when she didn't wake up, I thought it was odd. I was only 4 years old, and we shared a bed when I stayed with her. So, I sat up, reached over and kissed her on the cheek. After all, this is how Snow White had awoken from her sleep. But nothing aroused her.

My aunt came in later that morning, and being a nurse knew what had happened and what to do. She asked me to go to the other room and get dressed. A flurry of activity ensued with an emergency vehicle arriving with medics lifting her onto a stretcher, and taking her away.

The next time I saw her, she was lying in a casket, her arms crossed over her body with her hands on top of one another, a rosary entwined. I knew she was OK.

Several months later, she came to me in a dream. Grandma Michelina may have left the planet, but was with me in spirit.

So, what is it about death that frightens us? I encourage you to reflect upon that now. Make amends with yourself. Free yourself from the entanglement of fear. Write down a list of exactly what it is that you might be afraid of. Then act on it. For instance, if you're afraid of what happens once you die, research spiritual practices and religions until you find one that resonates with you. Join and study. See where it takes you.

Free yourself from the entanglement of fear

If you are concerned about leaving loved ones behind, look more deeply. What do you need to do or say in order to give both you and your loved ones' comfort at the time of your departure? Act on it.

Set yourself free by knowing what it is you are afraid of. Because conquering fear is not as hard as you think.

MEDITATION ON GROUNDING, TRUSTING & PREPARING

Take 3 deep breaths in and out releasing any tension held in your physical body.

Take 3 more breaths to release any tied-up emotions.

And on your final 3 breaths, clear your mind of thoughts. This includes ideas and to-do lists.

Feel your connection to Mother Earth.

Bringing your awareness to your feet, feel how grounded you are. Breathe right down to the soles of your feet and feel your connection to Mother Earth. Allow her to support you, to hold you, and to ground you into your physical body.

Now bring your awareness to your heart center right in the center of your chest. As you breathe from this center, feel the well of love within you. Allow it to ignite—like a flame being lit. With each breath allow yourself to relax, releasing the sensation of love throughout your body.

Focus on your heart center while you ask yourself what it is that you're afraid of when it comes to the idea of death. Notice what arises. Is it something concrete? Like a mortgage for your house? Does the image of a person come up? Who is it? What do you think they will need from you? Notice what shows up for you.

Then, ask yourself what unfinished business you still have that you would like to accomplish. Make a list if you'd like. Then take the top 3 and set them as priorities.

Take a deep breath right into the center of your heart chakra, and affirm that you will act upon the insights you have received.

Know now that death is inevitable. Whether today or many, many years from now. Ashes to ashes. Treat every day as a gift!

MINDFULNESS TIP OF THE DAY

Release fear of death by treating each day as a gift. Know that you have the power to act upon what really matters to you. Whether it's providing for a loved one, releasing debt, or pursuing a creative dream. Identify it and follow up with action.

MANTRA

"I am full of life and live each day as if it were a gift."

Alana Cahoon

JOURNAL YOUR INSIGHTS

Chapter 9

ANTI-AGING

BEAR IT

She felt alone
And had begun to change
These eyes once her greatest feature
Now framed with lines - crows feet
Crows feet for God's sake
And her pouty lips
Now furrowed
What on earth
Had happened
To her
Face
What had happened to her face
Wearing a permanent mask of
A lifetime
Worn out

Her body—hah!
That once tight fit & fab-u-lous body
Sagging ... here ... there
Everywhere
Aging
How is a modern woman to Do it!
Bear it
Live with it
A sculpt here. A tuck there. Needles
Everywhere
Sigh
What happened to the quiet (and dark)
Rooms of later age
Allowing the youth to run around (in daylight)
The elders held back
Nurturing the wisdom from the years of
Living
Salving the exposure to the
Sun
Healing the wounds of
The Soul
Being there
Just
There
Waiting to be needed
Not necessarily looked upon
But sought out
For comfort

Security
Love
Guidance
Wisdom

AGING GRACEFULLY

Youth is taken for granted. Unless you're raised on the stage or screen, at which point youth ends at a very tender age. But for most people, especially in the modern world, the 21st century, youth appears endless until it suddenly comes to a halt. That halt is called aging. If you're lucky, it approaches in stages.

"Oh my, what's this? A line on my forehead that won't go away."

Or—

"This belly has a mind of its own. No matter what exercise regime I engage in, it says—No, I'm staying!"

And then there are days when all at once you seem to have aged decades. You are tired, achy, pale, dry. Need I continue?

Here's the thing. You don't have to. You just don't have to.

You can age gracefully. Regardless of the tiny lines, the annoying furrows, the plump belly. You can age with dignity and grace.

Who says you're not perfect

Who says you're not perfect at the age of 30? Beautiful at 40? Ravishing at 50? Gorgeous at 60? Stylish at 70? Definitely a knockout at 80! And, hello—you're still here at 90? How'd you do it?

Allowing outside influences to tell you what you are supposed to look like will likely result in a disastrous attempt to change.

I say—let's move ahead together on a slower path of physical aging. I'll tell you what that means.

Meditation can help slow down the aging process. How, you may ask. Well, here are my thoughts.

When we meditate, we slow down and relax. All the muscles in our face also relax. There is no tightness in the jaw, the mouth, the forehead. Just a peaceful state of being.

Compare that to being engaged in an urgent project. The eyebrows come together feeding the furrows between them. The jaw tightens and the lips purse creating unwanted lines.

Or bring yourself to the scenario of preparing a family dinner with unruly children. You may find yourself yelling making all kinds of threatening faces!

On the other hand, the beautiful emotions of laughter, love and joy also contribute to wrinkles. These are usually found around the eyes.

And so, meditation provides a peaceful experience, allowing all the muscles in your body and face to relax. It promotes stress reduction, bringing us to the second reason.

Stress underlies many unfortunate health risks such as increased heart rate, blood pressure, muscle tension, digestive disorders, mental health issues. The list goes on. These impact your overall health which effects the aging process.

Stress underlies many unfortunate health risks

Have you ever heard of the expression, 'You're giving me gray hairs!' Or 'I just aged a decade.' These usually are directed toward teenagers. But not necessarily. It could be a difficult job, or any relationship involving an emotional upset.

Meditating on a regular basis will improve your ability to manage stress. This aids in slowing down the aging process.

*Meditating on a regular basis will improve
your ability to manage stress*

This aides in slowing down the aging process

When yoga accompanies meditation, your body receives the added benefit of muscle toning and bone strengthening. This keeps you healthy longer, feeling youthful, and full of vitality.

Now. That being said. There are certainly other means of counteracting the aging process. Here are a few I've learned along the way.

Stay out of the sun

Think about what heat does. It cooks. When you place your body under intense heat, you are literally cooking it! Does that sound good? No. So don't do it.

Drink plenty of water

Water is the fountain of youth.

Water is the fountain of youth

It purifies the insides from toxins such as processed foods (white sugar, bleached flour) and medicines (made of chemicals). Neither are easily digested by our bodies. While the needed properties may be absorbed, the rest are left behind, lining the internal body. Water is one way of washing your insides out like taking an internal shower.

Avoid smoking

In addition to the fact that smoking cigarettes can cause lung cancer, the act of smoking puckers your lips, attributing to lines being formed around them.

MEDITATION—FEELING BEAUTIFUL

Start by sitting on a comfortable chair or cushion.

Take 4 deep breaths in and out. With each breath, allow your shoulders to drop.

Relax your head and neck. Allow your back to be firm and relaxed at the same time.

Using your imagination, see a beautiful ocean in front of you. The sky is clear blue, dotted with soft white clouds. The sound of seagulls can be heard off in the distance.

Take a deep breath in and out. Allow yourself to sink into your cushion.

Imagine you are sitting on a sandy beach. It is both firm and soft. Holding you steadily.

Feel the sand under your fingers.

Breathe in now smelling the fresh clean air.

With your eyes closed, bring your focus to the crown of your head.

Imagine the sun, soft and luminous high in the sky above you. Sending rays of gentle light over you.

These rays feel wonderful. Like currents of healing energy.

Breathe in as they gently touch your head. Sending a wave of peace over your scalp. Flowing down your face. Relaxing every muscle in. Your forehead. Your temples. Your jaw.

Take a deep breath in and a releasing breath out as the sun sheds light over your throat, the sides of your neck. Flowing over your shoulders and down your arms and hands.

Breathing in feel the healing energy of the sun as his rays radiate down the back of your head, neck, and back.

Sun rays now pour down the front of your body, pooling around your hips, your legs and feet.

You are completely surrounded by brilliant rays of light.

Repeat this mantra.

"Breathing in I breathe in fresh clean air." "Breathing out I relax."

Bring your focus to your face and say,

"I am beautiful. I am young. I am wise."

And repeat it,

"I am beautiful. I am young. I am wise."

Continue repeating your mantra while feeling the rays of the bright sun radiate all around you. Feeling the cool sand under your fingers. Seeing the clear blue sky dotted with soft white clouds. Hearing the sound of seagulls off in the distance. And the gentle rhythm of the ocean.

When you are ready to come back, take a deep cleansing breath in and out, feeling radiant and refreshed!

MINDFULNESS TIP OF THE DAY

Meditation slows down the aging process. Being mindful throughout the day helps to manage stressful situations and to make wise choices. When you are relaxed and at ease, you feel better. When your emotions are calm, you feel beautiful.

MANTRA

"I am beautiful. I am young. I am wise."

JOURNAL YOUR INSIGHTS

Chapter 10

ABUNDANCE

LET IT BE

She spread out her arms and exclaimed
Let there be rain
And the droplets poured from the sky

He hammered his staff into the ground and commanded
Let the waters part
And like hair being parted down the middle of his scalp
A path was paved

He cemented his name on the bottom of the document
And a deal had been formed
Power Money Jobs

She sashayed down the runway
Purring with her seductive eyes
Selling swaths of designer styled fabric
With every swirl

He prayed every day fervently
Until his dad
Came home

THE POWER OF CONFIDENCE

Some people have talent. Some people don't.

Some people have brains. Some people don't.

Some people have confidence. Some people don't.

Which of these three: talent, brains or confidence, do you think is the most important to have in order to increase your odds of attracting abundance?

Confidence

You can be a brilliant painter but if you're not willing to share your work, it will never get seen.

You may be a mathematical genius, but if you're hiding out in your basement, your solutions may never serve the world.

If you're confident, however, whether your paintings are phenomenal or not, you are likely to succeed. Whether your intellect is above average or not, you are more likely to advance in a career of high achievement.

Confidence is a key component to attracting abundance.

How to generate it? Believe. Believe you can therefore you shall.

Believe you can therefore you shall

Believe in yourself! Believe in your mission. Believe you are worth it. And above all, believe the world needs you!

Believe. According to the dictionary, to believe means to accept something as true. In this case you are believing in yourself, and what you can offer to the world.

How do these two things activate abundance? When you believe in yourself, others tend to believe in you. When you believe that your gifts are necessary to the well-being of humankind, the world is more likely to believe they are, as well.

Another important aspect of the law of attraction is to be specific about what you want to attract. If it is a romantic love, define their gender, their values, their physical attributes, their nationality, etc. If it's a bike, note whether it's a mountain bike, speed bike or motorbike. The more specific you can be, the more closely a match your attraction is likely to be.

Be specific about what you want to attract

Remember, if you simply ask to attract abundance, you may attract everything including the kitchen sink.

Similar to how your gifts benefit the world, you will want to describe how your desired object of attraction will benefit the world when you have it.

For instance, once your ideal romantic partner comes into your life, you will be happier and more focused. In turn you will be more fun to be around, and productive at your place of employment. This serves not only you but many.

Once you get your 10-speed bike, you will exercise daily, improving your health and longevity. In turn, this will reduce the carbons in the air by not driving as often.

Let's begin.

Step #1
Believe in yourself

Step #2
Believe that you, your talent, genius, personality, gift, way of being—serves humanity.

Step #3
Identify something you would like to have.

Step #4
Explain how having this will benefit the world.

MEDITATION ON ATTRACTING ABUNDANCE

Close your eyes and take a deep breath in and out.
    Do this several times until you come into a state of calm.

"As I breathe in I relax."
"As I breathe out I let go."

Imagine the sun shining above you pouring radiant rays of light all around you.

Think of something you'd like. Something you don't have now.
See that as a person, a thing, an activity. Describe it in detail.

Visualize this desired attraction in front of you. As if it were real.
How does it feel? Describe that feeling.
Select one word to describe it. Remember it. This is your symbol.

Now. Imagine you already have your desired attraction, whatever it may be.
See yourself walking around with it. See yourself communicating with others. Notice how they respond to you. How does it feel? Remember this. It is your second symbol.

Now consider how this changes your life. Notice what feeling arises. Put it into one word. Remember it. This is your third symbol.

See how this attraction into your life impacts the lives of others. This may be your most important step. What is your word? This is your fourth symbol.

Now, place all four of your symbols together, side by side. Breathe them into your body.

This is your mantra.

When you are ready, come back to the present moment feeling refreshed.

MINDFULNESS TIP OF THE DAY

Be careful about what you wish to attract into your life. Consider how it will impact your current life, your friends and family. Ask how it will benefit not only you but humanity. When you are certain what you would like to have, be as specific as you can, and believe.

MANTRA

"I now attract my heart's desire.
It serves me and humanity."

JOURNAL YOUR INSIGHTS

About the Author

Alana Cahoon attended St Philip Neri Catholic School during her first six years of education. She discovered Transcendental Meditation as a teenager. At the age of 17, she became a vegetarian.

Ms Cahoon ventured to NYC with a bachelor's degree in theatre. She sprouted her wings as an actress, singer, songwriter. During her 10 year residence, she trained at the New York Open Center, a holistic learning facility. Shakti Gwain and Thich Nhat Hahn were a few of her influences.

After traveling the world, she returned to her home town in Upstate New York to raise her son where she became the Program Director of a technology business incubator.

Blending her creative skills with her holistic studies and business acumen, Alana founded Grow 2 B U Studios where she coaches clients to develop professional and personal balance.

Alana is a Certified Natural Health Professional, Yoga Teacher, Reiki Master Teacher, and Shaman. She is currently training in the Magyu path of Tibetan Buddhism at Tara Mandala under the direction of Lama Tsultrim Allione.

Learn more at www.AlanaCahoon.com.

Made in the USA
Columbia, SC
26 December 2022